ALL ABOUT ASIAN GIANT PANDAS

Carol Kline

Creating Young Nonfiction Readers

EZ Readers lets children delve into nonfiction at beginning reading levels. Young readers are introduced to new concepts, facts, ideas, and vocabulary.

Tips for Reading Nonfiction with Beginning Readers

Talk about Nonfiction
Begin by explaining that nonfiction books give us information that is true. The book will be organized around a specific topic or idea, and we may learn new facts through reading.

Look at the Parts
Most nonfiction books have helpful features. Our *EZ Readers* include a Contents page, an index, and color photographs. Share the purpose of these features with your reader.

Contents
Located at the front of a book, the Contents displays a list of the big ideas within the book and where to find them.

Index
An index is an alphabetical list of topics and the page numbers where they are found.

Photos/Charts
A lot of information can be found by "reading" the charts and photos found within nonfiction text. Help your reader learn more about the different ways information can be displayed.

With a little help and guidance about reading nonfiction, you can feel good about introducing a young reader to the world of *EZ Readers* nonfiction books.

Mitchell Lane
PUBLISHERS

2001 SW 31st Avenue
Hallandale, FL 33009
www.mitchelllane.com

First Edition, 2020.

Author: Carol Kline
Designer: Ed Morgan
Editor: Sharon F. Doorasamy

Names/credits:
Title: All About Asian Giant Pandas / by Carol Kline
Description: Hallandale, FL :
Mitchell Lane Publishers, [2020]

Series: Animals Around the World
Library bound ISBN: 9781680204049
eBook ISBN: 9781680204056

EZ readers is an imprint of Mitchell Lane Publishers

Library of Congress Cataloging-in-Publication Data
Names: Kline, Carol, 1957- author.
Title: All about Asian giant pandas / by Carol Kline.
Description: First edition. | Hallandale, FL :
EZ readers, an imprint of Mitchell Lane Publishers, 2020. | Series: Animals around the world-Asian animals | Includes bibliographical references and index.
Identifiers: LCCN 2018032701|
ISBN 9781680204049 (library bound) |
ISBN 9781680204056 (ebook)
Subjects: LCSH: Giant panda—Juvenile literature.
Classification: LCC QL737.C27 K58 2020 |
DDC 599.789—dc23
LC record available at https://lccn.loc.gov/2018032701

Photo credits: Freepik.com, Shutterstock, mapchart.net

CONTENTS

Giant Pandas 4
Where Do Giant Pandas Live? 22
Interesting Facts 23
Parts of a Giant Panda 23
Glossary 24
Further Reading 24
On the Internet 24
Index 24

4

The giant panda is a black and white bear. It lives in mountain **forests** in China. The forests are cool and wet.

Pandas eat plants and animals. Bamboo is their favorite food!

Bamboo is hard to chew. Pandas have strong jaws to chew bamboo. They also have an extra finger. The finger helps them hold the bamboo.

Giant pandas love to nap. They nap for two to four hours. They sleep on their side, back, or belly. They sleep in trees or where they feel safe.

Adult pandas are four to five feet tall. They weigh about 250 pounds. Their fur is very thick, oily, and woolly.

A female panda has five to eight **cubs** in her life. Cubs are born pink or white. They are born **blind** too.

Panda cubs cannot crawl until they are three months old. They stay with their mothers for two years.

Wild pandas are hard to find. Less than 2,000 giant pandas live in the wild. They want to stay hidden and alone.

Three hundred pandas live in zoos. Many zoos study pandas to help them **survive**. Pandas are important to the **culture** of China.

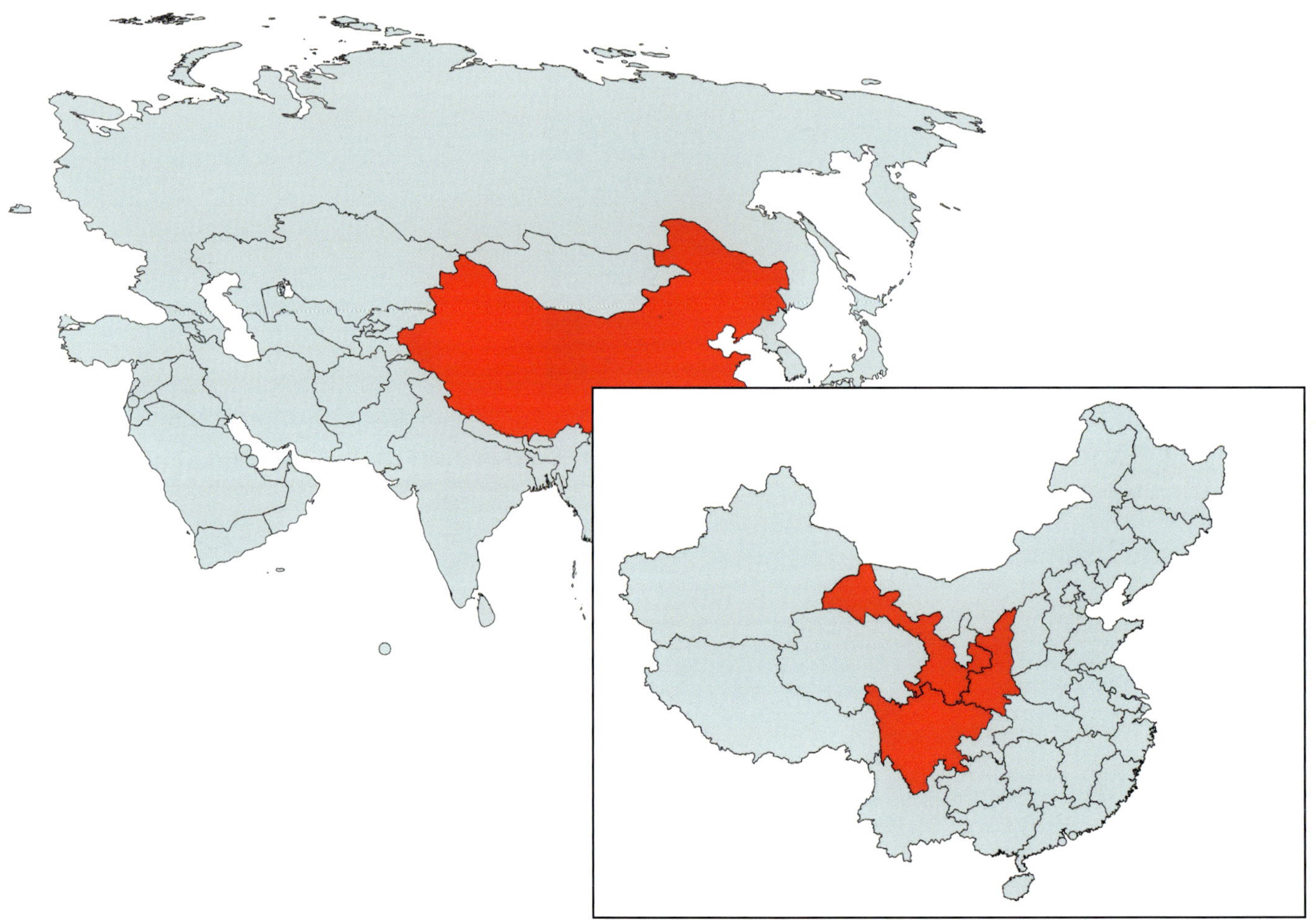

WHERE DO GIANT PANDAS LIVE?

China, specifically central China, in the provinces of Sichuan, Shaanxi, and Gansu

INTERESTING FACTS

- Pandas can live 20 years in the wild.
- Pandas eat grass, fruit, birds, and rodents.
- Pandas poop many times a day. They even poop when they sleep.
- Giant pandas make sounds when they play.
- Pandas sit on their bottom or lie on their back when they eat. Their back legs stretch out in front of them. They are good tree-climbers and swimmers.

PARTS OF A GIANT PANDA

Head
Pandas have big round heads, small eyes, and strong teeth. Their heads are white but have black rings around their eyes. Their ears are also black.

Teeth
Pandas have very sharp teeth for chewing tough bamboo.

Thumbs
Giant pandas have a sixth finger that is like a thumb. It helps them hold bamboo stalks.

Fur
The panda is well known for its black and white fur. Each bear has a different pattern of coloring.

Tail
Pandas have a very short tail.

GLOSSARY

blind
Not able to see

cub
Baby panda

culture
The habits or beliefs of a group of people

forests
An area with lots of trees

survive
To remain alive; to continue to live

FURTHER READING

Hanson, Anders. *Panda*. Minneapolis, MN: ABDO Publishing Company, 2014.

Thimmesh, Catherine. *Camp Panda: helping cubs return to the wild*. Boston: Houghton Mifflin Harcourt, 2018.

ON THE INTERNET

You can watch pandas on the Giant Panda Cam at the Smithsonian Zoo
https://nationalzoo.si.edu/webcams/panda-cam

For a four-minute video about Giant Pandas, visit this site.
https://www.youtube.com/watch?v=VNxx8jVEm3I

INDEX

Bamboo 7, 8, 23
China 5, 21, 22
Cubs 15, 17
Forests 5
Mountains 5
Zoo 21